DIVERTICULITIS COOKBOOK

A COMPLETE MEAL PLAN FOR DIVERTICULITIS AND ALL YOU NEED TO KNOW

DANEA HEFNER

Table of Contents

CHAPTER ONE

MEAL PLAN FOR DIVERTICULITIS

When trying to heal diverticulitis, what foods should you eat and which should you avoid?

Avoiding foods that can aggravate the pouches (diverticula) in your large intestine is the main goal of a diverticulitis diet. If you suffer from diverticulitis, adjusting your diet may help you manage your symptoms and avoid dangerous complications like bleeding and bowel obstruction.

Although following the broad strokes of a diverticulitis diet is a good place to start, you should also begin paying attention to how different foods make you feel. It's possible that you'll discover a link between your digestive issues and specific foods; this is information that you and your doctor or dietitian can use to create a diet plan that's just right for you.

Inflammation or infection of the digestive tract's small, abnormal pouches is called diverticulitis, and it is a common digestive disease. The condition known as diverticulosis is characterized by the formation of these pouches. After they become inflamed, the condition is known as diverticulitis. These conditions are also referred to by the term diverticular disease.

Doctor's Discussion Guide for
Diverticulitis

Get our printable guide to help you ask the right questions at your next doctor's appointment.

Benefits

Healthcare providers often recommend dietary changes to help manage diverticulitis, or even to reduce a person's risk of developing diverticula in the first place. This is despite the fact that every body is different and more research is needed to understand the relationship between diet and diverticular disease.

Changing your diet and other aspects of your lifestyle are among the few things you have any say over in preventing diverticular disease.

The main advantages of the diverticulitis diet are that it helps reduce inflammation and helps keep bowel movements regular.

Although you may reduce your risk of attacks by following this diet, there is no guarantee that you will be completely protected from attacks if you also engage in other pro-inflammatory behaviors. However, the fact that it may aid in alleviating symptoms makes it a worthwhile adjustment.

Eating in a way that aids in condition management while still getting enough calories and nutrients every day can be challenging.

Medical professionals have yet to pinpoint a specific cause for the formation of pouches in the intestinal walls. Some people believe that the strain on the digestive tract increases when fiber intake is low. If the intestinal walls are weakened, diverticula may form.

The condition is more common in people who eat a low-fiber diet (like those who follow a Western diet) compared to those who eat a high-fiber diet.

Constipation is something fiber can help with. One theory suggests that constipation raises the odds of developing diverticular disease.

As a result, it has been suggested that a higher fiber diet may help slow the progression of diverticular disease. Achieving and maintaining regular bowel habits can aid in the healing of an acute diverticulitis episode and the prevention of symptoms.

Evidence suggests that insoluble fiber may be particularly helpful for those with diverticular disease.

A minimum of 28 grams of fiber per day is recommended for adults consuming 2,000 calories per day.

Inflammation Down

The diverticulitis diet is aimed at minimizing the risk of inflammation in the digestive tract and relieving its symptoms if it does occur.

10 While avoiding or reducing certain foods may reduce your symptoms, medical professionals do not believe this will stop the progression of your condition.

CHAPTER TWO

Glucan, Beta-Glucan, and Inulin: Three Fiber Supplement Options

Mechanics of Operation

There are no strict regulations for this diet, but rather suggestions for what may help alleviate your symptoms and what may exacerbate them. If you have diverticulitis, you need to pay attention to your body and collaborate with your healthcare providers to figure out the best diet for you.

Eating less of something, or cutting out something entirely, could improve your health.

Duration

Your doctor may advise you to take it easy at the beginning of your fiber-eating or fiber-supplementation regimens. Gas and bloating can be avoided by increasing dietary fiber intake gradually from a low starting point.

How long you stick to your new high-fiber diet after you feel comfortable with it depends on your symptoms, the rate at which your diverticular disease progresses, other health conditions you have, and any other treatments you try.

It's possible that the positive effects of dietary adjustments will fluctuate over time. Digestion can be negatively impacted by age-related changes, for instance. Therefore, you may need to adjust or return to a diverticulitis diet at some point.

Insights Into the Functions of Your Digestive System

When to Eat What

There is no foolproof strategy for treating diverticulitis because the factors that contribute to the condition can be highly individual. Some recommendations may require trial and error, but there are some fundamentals that can help.

Legal Snacks

Fiber-rich foods

Bananas, apples, and pears

Foods like broccoli, carrots, and other root vegetables

What about some brown rice?

Products from seeds and nuts

Whole grains (oats, rye, and barley)

Supplemental fiber, such as psyllium husks

Olive oil and avocados are two examples of anti-inflammatory foods.

- Water

Those Foods That Don't Meet Regulations

Legumes (beans)

- Bran

- Cabbage and Brussels sprouts

Cultured foods

Fried foods

Dairy products with the full fat

• Onions, garlic

Red meat

• Soy

Trans Fats

It was once thought that eating foods like nuts, seeds, and popcorn could cause diverticulitis in those with diverticulosis, so they were generally avoided. New evidence, however, suggests that these foods do not directly trigger inflammation in the pouches. 11 Those foods are excellent fiber sources, so that's great.

Ginger, turmeric, and garlic are all spices with anti-inflammatory properties; ginger, in particular, is used as a folk remedy for settling upset stomachs. To the contrary, the digestive tract lining can be aggravated by spices. 12 After a severe case of diverticulitis, you might want to stay away from them. Then, begin with a low dose and gradually work your way up to your optimal intake.

Fruit: The fiber content of fresh fruits like apples is highest when the skin is consumed along with the fruit.

In addition to apples and pears, bananas are a nutritious fruit option. They are high in potassium and may aid in digestion, making them a good choice for those nursing an upset stomach. If you're experiencing the discomfort of diverticulitis, however, you should seek out lower-fiber foods like applesauce.

Cheese, yogurt, and milk with a low amount of fat should be included in your diet if you can digest dairy products. Full-fat dairy products can be difficult to digest even for people who aren't lactose intolerant. If you have diarrhea as part of your flare, you may want to hold off on dairy until you feel better. Cottage cheese and other low-lactose dairy products may be digestible.

Grains: Whole grains are a great way to get more fiber in your diet. When looking to increase your fiber intake, whole-grain options like bread, crackers, pasta, and brown rice can be a delicious and flexible choice. In contrast, when you're sick, it's best to eat things like crackers, rice, and white bread because they're low in fiber.

Whether you're experiencing symptoms or not, a high-quality protein source like lean ground meat or eggs can help. Nuts and nut butters, which are both high-fat foods, are another protein option. 14 When symptoms are particularly severe, they may not be the best option.

Avoiding unprocessed red meat may help you avoid diverticulitis, as this food group was found to be the most significant contributor to the development of the condition in one study.

Raw vegetables (especially root and cruciferous vegetables) are nutrient powerhouses if you are healthy and eating a high-fiber diet.

But you might want to stay away from them if you're experiencing any of the associated symptoms. You might find it difficult to digest a baked sweet potato with the skin on. Just use a white potato that you've peeled and mashed.

Drinks: Staying hydrated aids digestion of the extra fiber you eat and keeps you from feeling constipated. Stay hydrated by drinking lots of water and paying attention to whether or not other drinks (like coffee, tea, or alcohol) trigger or exacerbate your symptoms. In order to prevent further flare-ups, some people must permanently abstain from particular beverages.

CHAPTER THREE

Modifying Your Diet for Diverticulitis

Tell your doctor if you notice any adverse reactions to any foods. They can advise you on how to cut back or eliminate it without jeopardizing your nutritional status.

It's a good idea to discuss adding new foods (or ones you used to like) to your diet on a regular basis with your doctor. You can better control your diverticulitis symptoms by following a healthy and medically approved diet, but it's also crucial that you can actually stick to your diet plan. Over time, you may be able to gradually increase the variety of your diet without noticing any negative effects on your symptoms.

Recommended Timeframe

You should consider your mood and the realities of your daily schedule when making meal plans. Instead of sitting down to three square meals a day, some people with digestive disorders feel better if they eat smaller portions more frequently.

If you find that eating the same amount of food at the same time every day isn't working for you, try varying the types and amounts of food you consume throughout the day. You might also learn that some food combinations are good for you while others are not.

Be sure to include beverages in your meal and snack planning. Keep a water bottle close by so you can take frequent drinks throughout the day.

Advice on the Kitchen

For easier digestion, try cooking your food and peeling your fruits and vegetables. Carrots, potatoes, and apples all fare well once prepared in this way. You can make poached eggs instead of fried ones, and lean ground meat can be cooked until tender for protein.

Modifications

Dietary changes may help with diverticulitis management, but they may have unintended consequences for other parts of your health. Your diverticulitis diet may need adjustment if you also suffer from another medical condition, such as diabetes.

Low-fiber diets, in which refined white bread plays a central role, can help reduce inflammation and their accompanying symptoms. If you have diabetes, however, you should avoid foods made with refined flour because of the impact they have on blood sugar. 17

The way you eat may also need to be reevaluated if you've recently made significant changes to your lifestyle. Your nutritional needs will shift, for instance, if you are pregnant or nursing. Your nutritional needs may change if you engage in more strenuous exercise or if you're undergoing medical treatment for an illness, injury, or surgical procedure.

It's best to consult your doctor before making any drastic changes to your diet, including increasing your fiber intake or beginning fiber supplementation. Eating more fiber can exacerbate the symptoms of irritable bowel syndrome (IBS) and other gastrointestinal disorders. 18

Work with your healthcare team to ensure that the foods you eat are beneficial for both your diabetes and your other chronic health condition.

Gas, bloating, cramping, and other digestive symptoms can occur with dietary changes even in otherwise healthy people.

Typically, the soreness lessens as your body gets used to it. 19

Is There a Problem with Your Digestive System?

Before, During, and After an Incident

It may be necessary to allow your bowel to rest while experiencing or recovering from a flare of diverticulitis. However, many high-fiber foods that are usually beneficial for your condition may be difficult to digest while you're recovering from your illness.

Your doctor may advise you to consume less fiber, less residue, or even just liquids until you begin to feel better. The same holds true if you have diverticulitis and are dealing with complications like a bowel restriction (stricture) or infected pockets (abscess).

This short-term healing diet consists of 20 foods, including:

• Applesauce

• Broth

Cheese that isn't a block: cottage cheese

• Eggs

The Juice of Fruits (no pulp)

• Gelatin

Sorbets • Ice-Cream Bars

Lean meat that has been ground into a paste

Foods: • Potatoes (no skin)

Vegetables cooked to perfection

The White Bread

One type of rice that is commonly eaten is white rice.

To manage diverticulitis, you can gradually reintroduce foods until you're back to your regular diet.

Incorporate an elimination diet into your routine.

If you've got symptoms after getting a diagnosis of diverticular disease, your doctor may recommend going on an elimination diet. With this method, you wean yourself off of a problematic food or group of foods over time.

Once you've done that, give your body a few days to adjust to the new routine and make note of how you're feeling (usually over the course of a few weeks). At some point, you'll reintroduce the food in question and observe whether or not your symptoms improve.

CHAPTER FOUR

Considerations

You and your doctor should talk about possible treatments for diverticulitis. Your healthcare team may also benefit from the input of a nutritionist, among others.

Think about your current way of life, your budget, and your cultural preferences as you weigh your options. You and your doctor will work out a plan to make sure you're getting the care you need while managing any other conditions you may have.

Basic Dietary Maintenance

A diet high in fiber has many health benefits and can make you feel full for longer. If you're trying to control your symptoms by eating less fiber, you might find it difficult to feel satisfied on such a restricted diet.

Keep in mind that refined carbs like white bread and crackers can have a lot of extra sugar added to them. Gelatin and ice pops are two examples of liquid diet staples that can be high in sugar. These products don't do much for your body beyond keeping you hydrated.

Safety

Switching between high- and low-fiber diets has been found to be a safe method of treating diverticular disease.

20 Even among healthy individuals, the amount of fiber consumed on any given day can vary significantly.

Try not to make drastic changes at once if you're trying to reduce or increase your fiber intake to avoid the associated symptoms. Changes should be made gradually to allow your digestive system to adapt. 3

A sense of belonging and communal aid

Meeting up with others who also suffer from diverticulitis could be a comforting experience for you. Joining a support group, either online or in person, can provide a safe place to vent your frustrations and learn how others have found success in controlling their condition through diet.

Get in touch with your healthcare provider to learn about nearby options, and don't forget to look into support groups and forums online.

Cost

Low-cost, high-nutrient, high-fiber fruits and vegetables are abundant during the growing season. Rice and pasta, two staples of the diverticulitis diet, can be bought in large quantities at wholesale prices.

A doctor may suggest nutritional supplements or probiotics if dietary changes aren't enough, but keep in mind that these can add up quickly. Inquire if a prescription is required to obtain them, as this could increase the likelihood that your health insurance will cover the cost.

Impacts on Health

You may not feel as energized as usual if you are eating a restricted diet while recovering from an episode of acute symptoms. Alterations to your dietary routine may also cause shifts in your bowel routine.

In some people, increasing their fiber intake can cause digestive issues like flatulence and gas. Constipation is a possible side effect of drastically reducing your fiber intake. 21

Wellness in General

Make sure you're getting enough healthy calories every day, even if you have to eat less than usual to control your symptoms.

Some people find it difficult to eat because of their symptoms; in these cases, liquid nutritional supplements may be useful.

If you are nutritionally deficient or have trouble digesting food, your doctor may recommend that you take a multivitamin supplement.

Differences Between the Diverticulosis Diet and Other Plans

Diverticulitis diets are very similar to post-operative bowel rest diets, which are also commonly recommended. People with inflammatory bowel disease, both acute and chronic, and those recovering from a bowel obstruction can also benefit from these diets.

Eating on a BRAT Plan

You've probably heard of the BRAT diet if you've ever had food poisoning or your child has come home with a viral stomach bug. Eating a diet of soft but nourishing food can help alleviate symptoms like nausea and diarrhea while giving your digestive system a much-needed break.

The BRAT diet consists of refined white bread, rice, applesauce, and bananas.

The BRAT diet may help people with diverticulosis during an acute episode of diverticulitis or while they are recovering from surgery, but it is not sufficient for long-term management of the condition. When you're on such a strict diet, it's hard to get enough food to maintain your health.

Diet Low in Fermentable Short Chain Fatty Acids and Monosaccharides

The term "FODMAPs" refers to the various amounts of fermentable oligosaccharides, disaccharides, monosaccharides, and polyols found in the foods you consume. Foods high in FODMAPs cause some people to experience cramps, gas, and bloating. 23 Keeping track of how high-FODMAP foods affect your diverticulitis symptoms could prove useful.

CHAPTER FIVE

A Word

Your doctor may recommend adding supplements or medications like antibiotics to your treatment plan if you have other health issues or are not absorbing nutrients properly.

Keep in mind that everyone's physical structure is unique. The diet that works for you may not work for someone else with diverticulitis. For long-term health and well-being management, you may need to make dietary or other lifestyle adjustments.

REGULARLY INQUIRED ABOUT

When a case of diverticulitis flares up, how long does it typically last?

In most cases, symptoms of diverticulitis improve after only a few days of treatment. In some cases, they dissipate within a matter of hours. 24

The incidence of diverticulitis:

About 10% of people over 40 and 50% of those over 60 will develop diverticulitis at some point in their lives.25

Can you tell me about the causes of diverticulitis?

Age, being male, being overweight, eating a low-fiber or high-fat diet, smoking, and a lack of physical activity are all factors that increase the likelihood of developing diverticulitis. Some preventative measures against developing

diverticulitis include adopting a
healthy weight through diet and
exercise and giving up smoking.

9 798847 083287